650 | Immigration Nation

Edited by Edward McCann

650 | WHERE WRITERS READ

Founder / Editor • Edward Mccann
Executive Producer • Richard Kollath
Literary Ombudsman • Steven Lewis
Chief of Operations • Jane Kaupp
Technical Advisor • Conrad Trautmann
Technical Advisor • Stephen Kaupp
Director of Communications • Gretchen Reed
Director of Photography • Kevin O'Connor
Videography/Photography • Adley Atia, Sara Caldwell
Chief Audio Engineer • Jesse Chason
Copy Editor • Shelley Sadler Kenney
Graphic Designer • Diane Fokas
Production Director Emeritus • Gregory Bray

Production Assistants
Christopher Dennison, Diane Fokas, Mackenzie Meeks,
Jackie Mercurio, and Brian Reagher

Editorial Committee
Rachel Aydt, Laura Shaine Cunningham, Angela Davis-Gardner,
Joseph Goodrich, Steven Lewis, David Masello, and Honor Molloy

For our ancestors, and our descendants.

ABOUT 650

A quote on the wall at Ellis Island reads, "They told me America's streets were paved with gold. But when I got here, I discovered they weren't paved at all—and that they expected me to pave them."

Whether or not they imagined streets of gold, America's immigrants came to escape persecution, to join family who'd come before, and for the opportunities their hard work might afford. With the exception of Native Americans, virtually all 326 million residents of the United States are—or are descended from—immigrants. We present a few of their stories in these pages.

650 is a celebration of writing and the spoken word—a literary forum featuring two-page, 650-word personal stories that can be performed in five minutes. Our events at theaters, colleges, and libraries around the country are organized around single, broad topics that invite a range of expression, and recorded performances are added to a digital archive of writers reading their work aloud. The writers and their work receive additional exposure through podcasts, broadcasts, our YouTube channel, and in these printed volumes. The volume you hold in your hands is a curated collection from a select group of writers featured at a live reading at the New Rochelle Library in New York's Westchester County.

650 features graduate students and grandmothers, first-timers and bestsellers. It's all about the writing, with an emphasis on craft. It's about the choice of one word over another, about the shape of sentences and paragraphs, the arc of a narrative, the poetry of a unique literary voice. If you love language and enjoy a good story, you've come to the right place. To submit your work or attend our shows, visit our website or Facebook page, and join our mailing list.

Please tell your friends about us, and **spread the word about the spoken word.**

Ed McCann

Edward McCann, Founder / Editor

READ650.COM
FACEBOOK.COM/READ650

CONTENTS

650 | Immigration Nation

Edited by Edward McCann

MARILYN OGUS KATZ

Marilyn Ogus Katz taught in an educational opportunity program at the State University of New York at Purchase, and then served for many years as dean of studies at Sarah Lawrence College. She left academia to write; primarily fiction, and what had for Marilyn always been an exciting illicit activity, became a committed relationship with all of its joys and frustrations. Her essays on Wordsworth, the teaching of writing, issues in higher education, and the concerns of older women, have appeared in journals and anthologies. She completed a novel, *The Old City*, about a family of Latvian Jews caught between Hitler and Stalin in 1940 and 1941, and a collection of linked short stories, *A Few Small Stones*, about coming of age in an extended immigrant family in New York City during the 1940s.

A FEW SMALL STONES

Marilyn Ogus Katz

My cousin Harvey only calls when there's a death in the family. He's the custodian of our cemetery plot and must ask them to "open the grave," as though beneath the deceptive lid of grass, an empty space lies waiting.

Cousin Florence has died of a heart attack. Once again, Harvey suggests we drive out together. We haven't seen each other since the last funeral. But over sixty years ago, I babysat him as he toddled about, blond ringlets at his neck. Each mile on the Long Island Expressway takes us back to the past we share.

We grew up on that cemetery. Some families take pride in a homestead or a compound on a river. Ours struggled to preserve a patch of burial ground. In the 1930s, our grandmother and her five younger siblings, immigrants from Poland, bought a plot with sixty graves. They insisted we Jews own a piece of land from which no one could turn us away.

The family met on the first Saturday of each month in someone's home. Even as a child, I understood the difference between an uncle and a great uncle, a second cousin and a first cousin once removed. My grandmother held forth, her gold watch swinging like a pendulum below her waist. Bubbe, a leader at the Workmen's Circle,

1

could keep an agenda even in a room of boisterous brothers and sisters. Maintaining the cemetery plot was the first item of business, but the family also sent money to a sister in Poland, raised funds for the poor, planned the Hanukkah party and the annual picnic. Bubbe embraced the democracy of her adopted country and encouraged debate, but she always got her way.

We children fell asleep, snuggling among the abandoned coats on the bed, awakening overheated, and staggering into the night with imprints of coat buttons on our cheeks. When the great aunts and great uncles died, I visited our plot again and again, as easy around the gravestones as on the swings at the state park where we went for our picnics.

Harvey clutches the wheel and peers into the rain. I'm glad I brought my umbrella. His wife Cynthia died eleven years ago, my husband Mac, twenty. In the Jewish tradition, we will place small stones on their footstones today.

"What's with this strictly funeral relationship we have?" I say. "When I go, you'll have to introduce yourself and your children to mine."

"You were the best babysitter," Harvey says. "Remember that New Year's when we leaned out the window and banged pans against the sill?" But he doesn't promise to call between deaths.

We drive through the cemetery gates toward a dense skyline of monuments, so unlike the lawns of our childhood. When we step into the downpour, I don't recognize anyone except the husband of the cousin who died. We are a small family above ground.

The rabbi asks us to place a shovelful on the casket. The soil is drenched and heavy, the shovel hard to lift and turn. The thud and scatter of pebbles assaults the pine box again and again. When I bend to place the stone on my husband's grave, I long to laugh with him once more about these relatives who argued every month, as they

2

reached for roast chicken and potato kugel, about what shrubs to plant at the cemetery.

Now, only Harvey and I remember the aunt who knit sweaters with armholes too tight to move, the great uncle who paid for my mother's piano lessons, the cousin who ground gefilte fish each Passover, and Bubbe, who marched to demand the vote for women. Soon our family's cherished plot will fill with distant relatives who won't know or care about that once vibrant community of immigrants.

And Harvey will pull away from my corner with my drenched old umbrella on the floor of his car.

ANN CASAPINI

Ann Casapini has been a yoga and meditation instructor since 1995. A member of the Sarah Lawrence College Writing Institute community, her writing has been published in *The Sun, Intima: A Journal of Narrative Medicine, Weird Sisters,* and *The Afterlife of Discarded Objects: A Collective Storytelling Project.* She studies writing with Steven Lewis and lives in Tuckahoe, NY with her husband, John Gredler, and their son, Liam.

LA VIDA ES DIFICIL

Ann Casapini

Dora, my green eyed, Colombian, petite power-house-of-a-mom, is smart and practical: To get the odor off your fingers after chopping garlic, "Necesitas limon." Rub your fingers inside of a lemon. To chop vegetables, you must "Parate!" Stand, never sit, to prepare food.

To clean properly, you must use rags, trapos, not paper towels.

With all her beauty and "know-how," though, I often wondered why she always seemed to have a constant undercurrent of anger. I knew she'd left her family in Bogota when she was only twenty. But I didn't know why she was the first of her four siblings to come to the United States. I knew she struggled with English, and fought for everything she got, working in a cookie factory, as an elevator operator, a housekeeper and babysitter. But I didn't know why—even in the 1950's, when it was common for women to stay home after marriage—she was so adamant about having her own money, doing anything to be independent, still working while raising four children.

So I set up a tape recorder to interview her.

"My name is Isadora Tovar Sandoval. After my grandmother. I've always hated my first name. I prefer 'Dora.' I was born in 1925."

She looked away and fidgeted with her earrings before continuing. "I only went to the fourth grade because as the eldest, I had to work. My sister Mercedes was the lucky one. She completed high school. Learned typing. I had to earn money, washing other people's clothes in the river with my mother. I always felt I could do better than that.

"I wanted to help my family get out of poverty. We grew up with dirt floors. No running water or electricity until I was ten. Seven of us slept in one room."

I now knew what my mother was coming to the US for, but why was she angry?

"Your grandmother, su abuela, was only twenty when she had me. Yet she was very strict. One morning before school, she told me to loosen my braids and comb my hair while she went to get bread. I was too lazy to do it, so I just wet my hands and smoothed out my hair. When she returned she knew I'd disobeyed. She got so angry she picked up a stone and threw it at me as I ran down the street. It hit the back of my head, making me bleed. Mi Mama always had buen tino, good aim."

Was that it? But then Dora hesitated and looked at the floor. There was more.

She took a deep breath. "When I was born, my mama was not married. I was ilegitimo."

Part of me wanted to stop the recorder, to give her revelation some room.

But I pressed on: "So who was your father?"

"Antonio, your grandfather, was not my real father. My father's name was Moses Paez.

My papa would come to meet me after school sometimes, with little bakery treats for me. Papa died when I was seven. I tried once to ask Mama about it, but she refused to talk about him. I was brought up mostly by my grandmother; mi abuela, even after Papa died and Mama married Antonio and had more children. They often made me sleep at my abuela's house, away from my sister and brothers. I always felt separate."

Dora paused. Exhaled a long sigh. She cleared her throat. "La vida es dificil

"I was different. My skin was darker . . ." Her voice got deeper, angrier. "They called me Negrita.

ANGELA DERECAS TAYLOR

Angela Derecas Taylor writes about food and family dysfunction. A descendant of Greek and Italian immigrants, she was born and raised in a family restaurant business in 1960s Greenwich Village. Angela has traveled extensively, working for more than twenty years in the food and beverage industry, until her volunteerism and advocacy led to a mid-life career change into her current role as the executive aide to the mayor in New Rochelle. She has been published in The *Westchester Review*, a featured storyteller with 650, Pros(e) of Pie, and The Creative Breath, and has taken the stage at The Moth story slams in New York City. Visit Angela's website—FoodWineAndWords. com—for stories, events, and recipes.

ANGELINA'S

Angela Derecas Taylor

I was raised in Angelina's Restaurant, where I learned how to set a table before I knew my ABCs. Angelina's was my playground, the place where I spent my formative years with one foot in old world Italy and the other in bohemian Greenwich Village.

In the early 1900s, my namesake and maternal great-grandmother, Angelina Morra, came to America from the Piedmont region of Italy. She was illiterate, abandoned as an infant, and was raised in an orphanage with no formal education. When Angelina first arrived in New York, she found work as a scrubwoman, then as a laundress. Despite her lack of schooling, Angelina evolved into a shrewd businesswoman. She was "leaning in" long before it was fashionable in what was very much a man's world. She literally stuffed her mattress until she had enough cash to purchase a small rooming house on Greenwich Avenue. Then she sent for her twelve-year-old daughter, Emilia, and put her to work in the rooming house. A highly skilled seamstress, Emilia resented being brought here from Italy to work at menial labor, but she also idolized her mother's entrepreneurial spirit. In the 1920s Angelina ran a speakeasy and

9

when Prohibition was lifted, she opened Angelina's Restaurant and gave it to Emilia.

My grandmother, Emilia, had only a third-grade education but she inherited her mother's business acumen. Angelina's Restaurant was the foundation, "the roots," my grandmother would say, from which four generations of my family sprouted. It was also the beginning of what Emilia would turn into a small empire over her fifty-five-year matriarchal reign—three pieces of real estate and two successful restaurants on Greenwich Avenue—providing lifetime employment for her two sons and a daughter, my mother, Gloria, not to mention decades of culinary excellence.

I spent a lot of my early childhood in Angelina's where my mother worked as a waitress. I can still picture my grandmother, Emilia, who we all called "Ma," seated at the family table, polishing flatware and wiping out glasses, greeting her customers upon their arrival. Yes, the food was fresh and delicious, and my bartender-uncle made a fabulous *Old Fashioned*, but regular customers and tourists alike were predominantly drawn in for entertainment. Angelina's had a renowned legacy of open familial bickering, drunken drama, and behind-the-scenes scandal worthy of a television sitcom. If reality TV were around back then, my family would have been stars.

There's an old family story that goes like this:

Two women arrived at the restaurant. "This is the place I was telling you about," one said upon entering. "See, there's the father at the table; his son's behind the bar..." at which point Pa cut in to finish the woman's sentence " . . . and the Holy Ghost is in the back patio." He was referring to Ma, but did not realize she was right behind until she bopped him on the head.

"Good evening," she said, never breaking her warm and glorious smile. "Table for two?"

I would mimic Ma when I was in the restaurant, walking from

table to table, chatting with the customers, and was often invited to pull up a chair. The customers couldn't resist my stories—innocent revelations of family secrets. Shocked and delighted, they gave me their undivided attention, eyes wide and mouths open. Nervous and unsettled, Ma strained to hear me from the family table, twisting a napkin before summoning my mother in Italian, *"Get her away from my customers. She's telling them everything!"*

"AN-ge-la!" my mother sang. "Come here now. Don't bother the customers."

"Don't worry, mommy," I once called back across the crowded room. "I didn't tell them you say *F-U-C-K!*"

I reveled in the customers' adoring attention and laughter, even as my mother dragged me to the bathroom for a spanking.

ANNA GERALDINE PARET

Anna Geraldine Paret first came to New York as an investment banker transferred from London. She has lived in America for over twenty years—in Palo Alto, California, Washington, DC, and New York City. Anna and her husband currently live in Larchmont, New York. Their oldest daughter attends university in England and their youngest in Washington, DC. A former docent at Stanford University's Jasper Ridge Biological Preserve, Anna is presently a naturalist at Sheldrake Environmental Center in Larchmont. Her work has appeared in *Orbis #173, Inscape,* where she received the Editors Choice award for the poem, "What is the Grass?" and *Ghost Town Literary Magazine.* She is a 2016 Scott Meyer Award short story finalist.

I AM UK

Anna Geraldine Paret

In the 1980s, on a flight to America, we were required to fill in a form for the Immigration and Naturalization Service, infamous for its officious bureaucracy and its downright nastiness. We declared, with straight faces, that we had not obtained our visas fraudulently, and that we had never been involved in genocide. We were required to state our nationality. I am from England, a country in the United Kingdom of Great Britain and Northern Ireland. This means that I am English. According to my passport, my citizenship is British. The choice was clear: English or British, both were accurate.

I shambled off the plane and joined the long, static line of British nationals herded between a thick rope and the wall, waiting to go through Immigration. Ahead of me, a drama unfolded; voices were raised. A stunned-looking young woman clutching a heavy coat and an overstuffed carry-on bag, pressed back up the queue. "You have to put UK," she sniffed. "If you don't put UK, they send you to the back." UK is not a nationality.

"Squeeze in here," someone said, making space for her. Then I overheard a snigger and a stage-whispered, "unless you've committed genocide . . ."

Surprisingly quick for such a heavy person, a uniformed official appeared alongside them, on the other side of the rope. "No cutting," she growled. "Back of the line." We flattened against the wall to allow the young woman through.

"Take one and pass them along," we UK's said, as we handed a stack of replacement forms up the queue. "Anyone got a pen?"

Years later, I applied for American (I mean US) citizenship, a process which involves a test and an interrogation (I mean interview). A preppy professional in a mid-floor office in downtown San Francisco asked me to write a sentence in English. I must have looked blank because he said, "Oh I don't know, write, 'I am a mother'." I wrote, 'I am a very good mother', and passed.

An envelope waited on my assigned seat at the ceremony at the Masonic Center. It contained my personalized Naturalization certificate and a US passport application form. A Russian, dressed smartly in 1970s flares, sat on my left. The tiny East Asian woman to my right spoke such appalling English that I wondered how had she managed to write, 'I am a mother'. Perhaps she wasn't.

I felt like a fraud. I wasn't escaping financial or political hardship; I was naturalizing because I feared that one day a capricious president might revoke my so-called permanent residency status— want my green card back—and separate me from my family, my children. I wouldn't even have to give up my UK citizenship. I wanted to call two great countries home.

There was a shuffling, some coughs, as a pretty high schooler in a long, black dress took the stage. As she sang "The Star Spangled Banner," two thousand now-silent congregants squared their shoulders, proud of themselves. *Francis Scott Key*. It was on the test. A Japanese American woman, an elected official of the city, told us her grandparents' immigration story, welcomed us to the US, and reminded us to vote. An elegant Cuban gentleman in a cream suit and spectator shoes, two rows in front of me, stepped up to the podium, and expressed his gratitude to America. In unison, we pledged our allegiance.

After the event—after a representative had announced in broken English that the INS was hiring and that job interviews were being held in the foyer—I strode out of the hall, truly believing that there could not have been an occasion handled with more efficiency, warmth and grace than the ceremony hosted by the Immigration and Naturalization Service. A UK has never felt more welcome.

JUDITH HEPBURN BLANK

Judith Hepburn Blank is an award-winning writer, editor, producer, and host who worked for thirty years in both commercial and public radio and TV, including CBS, NBC News, WHYY, NPR and WNYC. Her writing has appeared in New York *Newsday*, *The Sacramento Bee*, *Columbia Journalism Review* and *Sesame Street Parents* magazine. She has taught english composition to college freshmen, has edited the writing of Pulitzer Prize winners and college interns, and has interviewed people (and Muppets) ranging from Jane Fonda to Elmo. She lives in Brooklyn with her husband, Vincent Pinto, and their amazing dog, Zeke.

COMING TO AMERICA

Judy Blank

I was always proud to tell the story of my grandfather, the Russian revolutionary. He bravely eluded the Czar's police in the dead of night by slipping across the Black Sea from Odessa into Turkey. He landed on Ellis Island in 1911, with his young wife, who was pregnant with my father.

That was pretty much all I knew about my Russian Jewish heritage.

There was so much more family history on my mother's side, the Scottish and English Protestants who came here between the 1700s and 1800s. The wealth of ancestral lore was almost overwhelming: family trees, my great-grandfather's diaries, even a book chronicling my Scottish progenitors, written by some great-uncles. And there were photographs. Albums and albums of photographs, as well as framed portraits on the wall above my mother's desk.

My father had no photo albums. How could he? His parents were immigrants who fled in the night. All I ever saw was a framed picture on his dresser: a group photo depicting his father as a teenage boy at a trade school for Jews. I wanted to know more.

My father said my grandfather was a Socialist revolutionary who, with his comrades, leaned out the windows of buildings and dropped bombs in front of the Czarist troops marching in the street below. They'd drop a second bomb at the rear, trapping the men, and then a third bomb right in the middle. No wonder he had to flee.

My grandfather was an enigma. In Russia, he'd been a freedom fighter—or a terrorist, depending on your point of view. But here in America he worked as a tool and die maker, raised a family of four children and lived in a comfortable house with a sun porch.

When I was sixteen my parents divorced and, shortly afterward, my father died. The past seemed closed to me. I lost my father and I lost touch with his family. But after thirty years, I found myself reunited with them in Cleveland, where he had grown up.

Suddenly, my immigrant family came into view. There were photo albums after all, full of pictures taken in Russia, Germany, and France. One cousin they called *The Rota*, The Redhead. Another was a well-known singer. My grandfather was handsome in his youth. There was a family history.

I learned more. My grandmother was an expert seamstress. My grandfather was not just a tool and die maker; he invented the swing-top trash can. Offered a job as a designer in Chicago, he moved his family there, saw a sign at the factory gate announcing "No Jews," and went back to being a tool and die maker in Cleveland.

A few years ago, I got in touch with my father's French cousin, Eugenie, who lived in a suburb of New York. My father helped her come here after World War II and she adored him.

We spent hours exchanging stories. As she filled in the family tree for me, the yin and yang of my WASP and Jewish backgrounds felt more balanced. At one point, I mentioned my grandfather, the socialist, escaping the Czar's police. I had always wondered if the story of the brave revolutionary escaping in the nick of time was a complete fabrication—something said to impress his children, perhaps—or if it really did happen. I had learned it was certain that as a sixteen-year-old, during the pogroms of 1905, he acted as a messenger for the resisting Jews. But when I asked about the daring escape, Eugenie's eyes grew wide. She started to speak. She hesitated. Her mother was my grandfather's sister and she knew all about his flight from Odessa. "Oh, yes!" she said, about to put everything into perspective, "Your grandmother was pregnant when they arrived here." She paused. "But they weren't married. That's why they ran away."

MIHAI GRÜNFELD

Mihai Grünfeld was born in Cluj, Romania where he lived with his family until he was eighteen. In 1969, he and his older brother traveled to Czechoslovakia and from there escaped to Austria. Thus began a long journey that took him to Israel, Italy, Sweden, and Canada in search of a home in the West. Eventually he settled in the United States, obtaining his PhD from the University of California at Berkeley. Since 1987, he's been a professor of Spanish and Latin American Literature at Vassar College. Published books include a 2008 autobiography, *Leaving—Memories of Romania,* and *Antologia de la poesia latinoamericana de vanguardia.* An unpublished novel was adapted into a 2017 play entitled *The Dressmaker's Secret,* which enjoyed a sold out run in New York City. He lives with his family in Poughkeepsie, New York.

ACROSS THE BORDER

Mihai Grünfeld

My brother Ferkó and I board the seven o'clock train for Vienna and settle in a cold and empty compartment. We try to be inconspicuous and act like passengers accustomed to traveling, but I am just eighteen, poor, unwashed and unshaven. My pants are wrinkled and I have a toothache. We left Romania two weeks ago and this is the last step in our escape: getting from Bratislava, in Czechoslovakia, to Vienna, in Austria.

Our train starts off slowly, as if telling me that I must be patient. We change tracks in a small, deserted town with just a few snow-covered houses. Then we go ahead for a few minutes. Then back. Across from me, Ferkó is reading, calmly. He wet and combed his hair this morning in the bathroom. In his dark suit and barely wrinkled shirt, he looks as tall and handsome as ever. I settle down somehow, cuddle up in the corner, covering my face and my pain with the thick, window curtain.

Voices awaken me. A tall guard dressed in a green uniform speaks to us. My brother hands both passports over. The guard has wide shoulders, light blue eyes and a square, powerful jaw. He takes the documents and looks at them, page by page, examining them carefully. His face is frozen. He glances up, takes a step towards me and moves the curtain that has been partly covering my face. I point to my swollen jaw. He just looks at me, then returns the passports to my brother and leaves the compartment with a short army salute.

"What's happening?" I ask, trying to breathe again. Through the hall windows, I catch a glimpse of several armed guards going along the train with a huge German shepherd, looking under it.

Suddenly, I feel the jolt of the train taking off. Through the window, the telephone poles are passing us, wires going up and down, up and down. I can hear the rhythmic sound of the wheels, beating like my heart and, all of a sudden, the realization comes to me: We must have crossed the border.

Ferkó's dear, familiar face slowly breaks into a smile, a long smile. I stand up and hug him. We are laughing nervously, turning around on one spot like a slow top.

A few moments pass. Then, I do not know what to do anymore, and look through the window, hungry for a different landscape. I want to see something that tells me that I am free, that a completely new life is starting for me. I see fields and fields covered with fresh snow, broken up every now and then by dark clumps of trees. Nothing looks different. Though, when I pay closer attention, I notice that the houses in the distance are large. It doesn't make sense that country houses owned by peasants are several stories high. This is it. A wave of well being comes over me.

I am eighteen, on the train to Vienna, and the world is opening up for me. Once there, I can do whatever I want. I can work and make lots of money. And I can travel anywhere. Then, a new question creeps up: What exactly are we going to do in Vienna? It is the middle of January; we have very little money and do not know anyone. I look out the window: farm houses, country roads and cars. My tooth does not hurt anymore. We eat some stale bread and two apples. The combination tastes delicious. I think of Vienna, of being in the street and walking without any destination. I am excited and don't want to fall asleep and miss anything. Ferkó and I chat a little but soon fall into a contented silence and let time go by as the monotonous landscape unrolls before our open eyes.

STEVEN LEWIS

Steven Lewis Literary Ombudsman for 650, is a columnist at *Talking Writing*, and a member of the Sarah Lawrence College Writing Institute faculty. A longtime freelancer, his work has been featured in *The New York Times, The Washington Post, Christian Science Monitor*, the *Los Angeles Times, Ploughshares, Spirituality & Health,* and other publications. His novels include *Take This* and *Loving Violet*, both from Codhill Press. Finishing Line Press published Steve's poetry chapbook, *If I Die Before You Wake*. His backlist includes *Zen and the Art of Fatherhood, The ABCs of Real Family Values, The Complete Guide for the Anxious Groom,* and *Fear and Loathing of Boca Raton (a Hippie's Guide to the New Sixties)*. He divides his time between his writing space in New Paltz, New York and Hatteras Island, North Carolina.

AN IMMIGRANT FROM
THE BOROUGHS

Steven Lewis

All that is left of moving day 1951 is a curled black and white snapshot with scalloped edges. It's hard to tell which is more spindly, the bare maple tree that came with the new ranch house or me, the skinny, big-eared four-and-a-half-year old standing in front of it.

We had moved from 135-18 Seventy-seventh Avenue in Queens to this potato farm bulldozed into a housing development in distant Nassau County. Our family back in the boroughs felt we had crossed international boundaries and deserted them all.

A week before that historic migration, I had tripped on the concrete steps of our apartment building and began howling. My Aunt Miriam, who would later follow the wagon train across county lines to her own plantation-sized 100 x 100 foot plot of land in wild and woolly Great Neck, soothed me by saying there would be no steps at my brand-new ranch house in the country.

She was right. There were no steps. No sidewalks. And the narrow roads in the development were not yet paved. We didn't even have telephone service. A temporary booth was installed on the corner of Bluebird Drive for emergency calls. This was wilderness and we were brave settlers.

Most amazing to this undersized refugee from the world of numbered avenues, elevators, and honking traffic, my street was named Candy Lane. Did I think that candy canes would grow on that spindly tree, like on the Candyland game board? Absolutely. Did I know then that I would later spend my college days in mortal fear that anyone would find out that I grew up on Candy Lane? No.

And thus the universe was full of possibility for me. As it was for our parents who had courageously cut their tap roots so that their children would know the postwar bliss of crickets, crab grass, barbeque grills, chartreuse dinette sets, two car garages, and pink mohair sweaters.

Sixty-seven years later, though, with seven kids and sixteen grandchildren riding my shoulders, I am by necessity not spindly anymore. And, as I found on a sentimental journey downstate last summer to the old quarter-acre homestead, the maple tree is long gone.

Nineteen Candy Lane looked like a graphic off a Scott's grass seed box: a weed free carpet of lawn right up to a perfect flagstone path, manicured yew bushes in front of a nondescript grey house that bore only a passing resemblance to the tract home I grew up in.

No one was on the street that afternoon. No punchball games. No marbles. No bikes tossed onto the lawns. No one working under the hood of a car. The great sense of renewal and possibility had been long ago photoshopped out of this scene. Little left to recall that the original second generation Eastern European Jewish settlers to this rural outpost—the Schnippers, the Weils, the Danzigers, the Formans, the Diamonds—ever raised kids here.

And by the time I drove out of that unfamiliar upscale development, I understood that it no longer takes courage or moxie to make the trek to Roslyn Heights, just a hefty down payment and a contract with United Van Lines.

But in February 1951, with a dusting of snow on the grassless lawns along Candy Lane, everything was as bright and shiny for this immigrant boy as the bulb that magically lit when I opened our brand-new GE refrigerator.

DAVID J. KOZLOWSKI

David J. Kozlowski is a lawyer, father, husband, child of the '80s, and pop culture nerd who enjoys following sports and politics. His writing can be found on The Huffington Post and the *Good Men Project*, among other places, and he's a former columnist for the New York *Daily Record*. Dave strives to make a positive impact on the world. To that end, he serves as Editor-in-Chief and a member of the Board of Directors of Peace Love Progress.com, a nonprofit website dedicated to sharing true uplifting and inspiring stories of compassion and personal growth. He is also a Board Member of Pronto Comics, a nonprofit comic book company focused on helping writers and artists break into the industry. Dave also volunteers at the legal clinic for the LGBT Bar Association of Greater New York.

A ROCHY HISTORY

David J. Kozlowski

My oldest child is seven. He's learning about Ellis Island in school, so he wants to know where he comes from. My father-in-law has the history of my wife's side of the family, and my maternal grandmother, ninety-one and sharp, can share what she recalls of our Slovak family's emigration.

But there's scant information about my dad's lineage—and even less that I'm willing to share with him right now. Here's what he'll hear about his great-great-grandfather: Roch Kozlowski was born in Poland in 1889. As a young man, he came here, got married, and had eight kids. Imagine how busy their small house must have been! He worked in a brass foundry and was a part-time bootlegger—I'll explain when you're older. Once, there was an accident in his house and everyone almost died. They survived, but the story was on the front page of the newspaper!

One of Roch's children was named Walt. He was my grandpa, who fought for our freedom in a war. His son, also named Walt, is my dad. You call him Papa. Papa was the first in this family line to graduate from college. He had me, and I got married and had you.

That'll be it. For now.

Along the way, I have gleaned a few more details: My father tells me Roch made bootleg liquor during Prohibition, and he went blind in 1952, about when my dad was born. My grandfather would visit Roch with my dad. Roch would rub my dad's head and tousle his hair to feel how tall he'd gotten. Then, Roch and Grandpa would chat in Polish until it was time to leave.

Roch died of tuberculosis before I was born. Only one of Roch's children is still alive, my great-aunt Helen. She says Roch emigrated from Poland around 1910 to avoid mandatory military service. He married, had eight kids, and owned a popular speakeasy during Prohibition. Unfortunately, Aunt Helen's memory suffers. Her uncle—Roch's brother—owned a saloon, which I think she conflates with Roch's bootlegging.

Then there's the story older generations swear is true. They say there was a gas leak in Roch's house in the early thirties that almost killed the whole family. It led to complications that claimed the life of Roch's seven-year-old daughter, Dorothy, whom he called Dottie. The old folks say the ordeal appeared on the front page of *The Bridgeport Post*. My search of newspaper archives found nothing. I assume faulty memories, but accept the blame of poor research technique.

With some of my own research, I have learned that Roch successfully avoided the military, but did fill out a draft card for World War II. From it I learned his middle name—Zigmund—and birth date, August 16, 1889. It told me he stood five feet, six inches and weighed 200 pounds, with a ruddy complexion, gray eyes, and head full of brown, graying hair. I have one picture of him. It's black and white and yellow. Roch looks like a portly version of Grandpa.

The 1910 Census lists his occupation as "love maker" in a "factory." I chalk this up to my poor reading of century-old script, not an actual job title. By 1930, his position was "moulder" in a "brass foundry," and a decade later, in the last Census publicly available, "moulder" in a "machine shop." In 1954, according to *The Bridgeport Post*, he was a pallbearer. Twice.

Most of that I'll save for my son until he's older. But for now I'll add, "If Roch were alive today, he wouldn't be able to see you, but would reach out and tousle your hair and comment in Polish on how big you're getting."

TERESA LA GRECA

Teresa La Greca worked as a project director in medical publishing, a position that enabled her to travel throughout the US, Europe and as far away as Australia. Intrigued by languages, she welcomes the opportunity to practice when visiting relatives in France, Italy, and Greece. She enjoys reading, swimming, and long walks, and is an avid yoga and Pilates enthusiast. She's currently working on a family memoir that delves into World War II and the immigrant experience.

EXCEPTIONS TO THE RULE

Teresa La Greca

My Italian father found the English language daunting, even though as a soldier in Greece he had learned to speak Greek, fluent enough to pass for one. He would often say, *"La lingua inglese e una lingua bastarda"* (the English language is a bastard language). He recognized long before I would that English is comprised of French, German, Greek, Italian, Latin, among other languages, that made pronunciation of many words inconsistent and a guessing game for foreigners and even Americans.

At a moving-up ceremony at the end of our second school year, I was eight and my brother, six. Principal Cagan walked us onto the stage introducing us and telling the audience of the remarkable progress we had made. She went on to say that we had worked hard and now spoke English with barely a trace of an accent. We worked hard, eager to learn our new language and to fit in. It wasn't always easy and there were a quite a few bumps along the way. Our teachers were very supportive encouraging us, giving us books to read over the summer. Our mother read with us enabling her to learn as well.

That first summer in America, we came across the word

"laughing" in our books and pronounced it "lau-ging". It didn't sound right to us but we couldn't think of another way to pronounce it. When we returned that September the word appeared in a passage I was reading aloud. The teacher corrected my pronunciation and told me what the word meant. All excited I ran home and told my mother. "Are you sure?" she asked, "There is no *f*?"

I told her that the letters *gh* are pronounced like the letter *f*.

It was a great joy to be able to pronounce the word correctly after mispronouncing it all summer long. I later learned that the letters *ph* in the word photograph are also pronounced like the letter *f*. This confused me very much. I wondered if wouldn't be better to spell the word like the Italians do: *fotografia?* This would make it easier for anyone to pronounce, even a non-Italian.

Throughout my early school years, I came across many exceptions to the rule. When I was in the fourth grade, I pronounced the word 'vegetable' as 'vege-table.' The teacher, stopped me and instead of correcting my pronunciation, she screeched in her ear-splitting voice, "Were you raised in a barn?"

I still remember Mrs. Taub because unlike my other teachers who were always supportive and kind, she was not. I don't remember ever seeing her smile, which made me think she was not happy being a teacher. Years later when I saw the wicked witch in *The Wizard of Oz*, I immediately thought of Mrs. Taub, except that Mrs. Taub was not green.

I was taken aback and didn't have a clue as to what a barn had to do with the word vegetable, but I sensed by her tone that I must have done something wrong. Many in the class, including the boys, rose to my defense telling her that I was doing pretty well for someone who had come America not very long ago. My classmates' response to that unkind teacher warmed my heart.

Some years later, reading aloud again, I came upon the word

"Colonel" and I pronounced it as it was written: "Co-lo-nel". The teacher smiled and said, "I can understand why you would pronounce the word that way, but that the correct pronunciation is 'kernel'."

Certain that she was reading on the wrong line I said, "But there is no *r* in the word."

With a kind smile, the teacher replied, "That's one of those exceptions."

Another exception. Like that witch, Mrs. Taub, who would have done well to eat her vege-tables.

ANTHONY MURPHY

Anthony Murphy is originally from Lancashire, England, and now lives in Yonkers, New York. He's Associate Producer of the spoken word event Rimes of the Ancient Mariner in downtown Manhattan. Nominated for a Pushcart Prize 2017 for work that appeared in *The Westchester Review*, he's the author of the mixed-up book of poems and prose, *Scoppetry*, available on demand. His graphic poem, "Liberty Takes a Break," is available at choice bookstores. Murphy curates the online time travel blog *Where The Wurms Play Rugby*, a space for tales of place and time.

WE'RE NUNS

Anthony Murphy

I am on a boat full of them. Novices anyway—is what they tell me. Out of habit.

I haven't had sex for a month, I am thinking, me too. But I was making polite chat when I asked what they all did for a living.

The novices had been noisy and full of themselves, and I was a party to it by proximity. We sat on the floor together because the Dublin ferry was so busy that all the seats had been given up to the infirm. It was a choppy crossing.

Nuns? They shut me down with that shocker so I contented myself with a can of beer. One of them wanted a quieter word though. She waited for the attention to tangent itself before she isolated me.

"What's the matter?" she asks.

"Not much." I lift up the urn and show her. "Ash! No matter really, just my dad."

I'm drunk and she knows.

"He needs an introduction," I say, as I pat the urn, to make her feel more included.

"I'm Fiona, pleased to meet you," she says, shaking the urn like a hand.

"This is Joe."

"You going to drink all of those?" She points out the case of Stella I had purchased from the duty free nestled between my knees.

"Not possible. Would you like one?"

"Nnnnn!" she shakes.

I offer what I am cradling to her friends then. "You?"

Her girlfriends seem offended that I've entered into their auras once more, but they take a beer each anyway.

"Don't you think you've had enough?" Fiona says.

"Not yet."

"How would you know?"

"I wouldn't."

"When do you stop?"

"When I do."

"Does it hurt?"

"Doesn't everything?"

"Jesus heals. He's there for you."

I don't know if she's having me on.

"He's there for you," I say.

"For all."

"How would you know?"

"Because he is."

"Just because?"

"Yes" she says.

"I've been Godless since I was eight. Have a beer!"

She shakes again.

"We've just come from a choir competition."

"How was that?"

"We won, thanks for asking!"

I see a unity in them, a sureness, they're a big-toothed grin of a team.

"Well done." I drink.

"We're celebrating."

"Doesn't look like it." I say.

"You don't have to get . . . listen . . . come with me."

So I go with her, I have to take my dad, up the carpeted stair onto the top deck. She holds the urn whilst I pull at the wind-stuck, leaden door. We look out for a while. The whole world is dark silver. Then, there, in the howl, and staring at the waves in the dark, she kisses me. I don't know why.

"Where are you going?" Fiona asks me, even as I stand there.

"I'm taking him back."

"Home." She flexes her neck.

"Yes."

I put the urn down between my feet so that I can free my hands. She kisses me more. It's a big snog.

We promise each other some more sunrises as we see the land we look for. She glows in the beauty of the morning. It must feel good to be going home, to belong. It's my first time here in years. I suddenly feel like a tourist in a familiar place that has grown without me. I break away from her and apologize.

We just stand there, in our own wake. It's awkward. She starts to shift from foot to foot after a while.

"It was nice meeting you."

"It was nice meeting you."

She goes back down to find her coven as we dock.

I give everyone some space, the last on deck again. When I descend it is through some squegging emotions. I know that they weren't nuns, and that they've drunk all my beer. My dad rolls about the ship in his new plastic house, laughing his lid off.

ELLEN NENNER

The progression of **Ellen Nenner's** life has taken her from music student at the High School of Music & Art, to piano student at The Juilliard School, to an economics/philosophy major at Mount Holyoke College, and finally to an MA in Urban Planning from the New School. Formerly a writer and editor at the consulting behemoth McKinsey & Company, Ellen has attended writing workshops at the Fine Arts Work Center in Provincetown, Massachusetts. She's a trustee on the board of MasterVoices, a not-for-profit performing arts institution that believes that the human voice is the world's most powerful instrument. Music is Ellen's great passion and she has found a profound connection between telling stories through music and telling stories through the written word. She is currently working on a non-fiction book of connected essays and short stories.

THE GREENER

Ellen Nenner

I am in my garden in Truro, a small town wedged between Wellfleet and Provincetown on the Outer Cape. September has brought its usual cool weather. I have started to convert the house from the locus of dinner parties and family visits. From a vacation option for widowed friends not yet comfortable or smart enough to reach out to live what's left of life, to a state of suspension: all systems off, bird feeders collected, washed, and put in the lower basement. The house will now sleep until early next May.

I spend some time pruning and tidying what is left of my heirloom tomato plants. There is nothing healthy or alive now, no fruit, only wasted bodies with thin, scrawny arms and stems so weak and dehydrated that they no longer have the strength to remain upright. So why am I bent over, snipping here and there, making things neat, sprucing up plants whose lives are spent?

I am thinking of another day, another time. I am at home in New York, standing in Ray's clothes closet, deciding how I should dress his body. He is in the funeral home, awaiting my decision. The casket will be closed. Our daughters, Jackie and Lisa, have already

41

said their final goodbyes at the hospital. Who would see him? Who would notice what he wore? But I want him to look every bit the "Polish Prince," a name my college friends dubbed him when we began to date seriously.

I pace back and forth in the closet, sliding the heavy walnut suit hangers he preferred back and forth, stopping in front of this jacket or that suit. I remember the pains Manny, the head fitter at Paul Stuart, took to ensure that the fit of his jackets was perfect. He knew just how much padding would equalize the one inch difference between Ray's right and left shoulders, the cost of carrying his heavy medical bag on eight to ten house calls a day. I finally select a navy blazer with beautiful gold buttons, a blue and white striped shirt, and a crimson, blue and white paisley tie. I always had the last word about the shirts and ties.

Ray was a Polish immigrant and a Holocaust survivor. After he was liberated from a Nazi concentration camp, he was sent to a displaced persons camp outside of Munich. He attended Ludwig Maximilian University's medical school in Munich, graduated in 1950, and immigrated to the United States.

When he came to New York, he spoke very little English and understood even less. Two or three movies a day taught him enough to pass the exams he needed to continue his medical studies. But the English language continued to trip him up for the forty years we were married.

"Sometimes the words just don't make sense. I remember Mort Green and his wife inviting me to dinner at a fancy restaurant," he said, smiling at the memory. "Mort had more house calls a day than any other General Practitioner in Queens, and he let me cover for him on the weekends. I needed the money and I needed that dinner too."

"I suppose I was what people called a 'greener' — meaning an unrefined, newly arrived immigrant. A lot of the food on the menu was unfamiliar to me until I spotted halibut steak. I absolutely knew what steak was."

He laughed, remembering how he forced himself to eat the fish—a food he avoided throughout our marriage. So why am I bent over, snipping here and there, making things neat, sprucing up plants whose lives are spent? Because words sometimes just don't make sense.

MALKA MARGOLIES

Malka Margolies grew up in Kansas City and resides in the Bronx. A graduate of both Brandeis University and Northwestern University, she is a former publishing executive who has worked at Random House and Book-of-the-Month Club. Favorite authors to collaborate with and read include Diane Ackerman, Gay Talese, Allan Gurganus, Maya Angelou, Eric Van Lustbader, Michael Pollan, and Clarissa Pinkola Estés. At CBS News, she was press representative for *CBS Sunday Morning with Charles Osgood* and *48 Hours*. She has published several essays over the years, including one in The New York Times about the West Side development in Manhattan put up by the current occupant of the White House. Most recently she served as communications director at The Hebrew Home for the Aged in Riverdale and currently works as a freelance publicist.

A SHARED NAME

Malka Margolies

When I first stood at her graveside decades ago on a cloudless day with the hot Israeli sun beating down on my bare arms and shoulders, my eyes were transfixed on the letters carved out so crisply on her tombstone. I was staring at my own name—and the month and date of her too early death at age fifty-six, etched underneath *our* name, was eerily close to my birthday. Recently I turned fifty-seven. I had never believed I was destined to live longer than her. Now I have.

My maternal grandmother, after whom I was named a decade after her death, remains a mystery to me, even though my beloved late father spoke of her often and always with a hint of sadness in his voice.

Here's what I do know about her life. Malka Margolies was a sixth generation to be born in what is now Israel. Her father died young in the 1917 flu epidemic leaving her mother in poverty with eight children to raise. Malka's mother, my great-grandmother known as the Bubbe Mushke, a direct descendant of the founder of the Lubavitcher Hasidim (a far cry from my own religious practice), died only two years before her daughter. My grandmother, who married

45

my grandfather at age seventeen moved to his native Jerusalem and came to America in January 1930, a few months after Arab rioting forced her to flee her home with her young children. She departed from the port city of Haifa where, along with four of her children, including my eight-year-old father, they boarded a rickety old Greek ship named *The Lord Byron*. They joined her rabbi husband who was already living in New York with their eldest daughter, my late Aunt Rivka. The youngest of my father's siblings, now also long since gone from this world, was born when my grandmother was already not well, and she was her only "Yankee" child.

I have nothing tangible from her. No Sabbath candlesticks, no pieces of jewelry, not even a postcard with her handwriting. What I have is a photograph of her that sits on my desk. She is standing in front of a nondescript brick apartment building in the Bronx holding the only grandchild she would ever know. She looks tired and worn.

She was in poor health most of her adult life and died in Atlantic City, worlds away from her birthplace in the port city of Jaffa, then part of Palestine. Her death certificate states she died of a "coronary thrombosis." She, along with my grandfather and father had gone to a hotel in Atlantic City for Passover because my grandmother was already too ill to prepare for the labor-intensive holiday. It was to be a vacation. For her it turned into an eternal one.

My grandmother never wanted to be here. She always longed to go home. Eventually she did—however not how she had imagined, but rather in a wooden box on a long flight before the days of jet travel—accompanied by my father in 1949, the only member of the family to fly back to Israel to bury her.

My father once told me that after they arrived in America, she would always remind him of their roots. "Moishele," she would say, "We came over to Eretz *Yisroel* (the land of Israel) on the Mayflower!" My father told me it was her way of telling him the family's roots in

Israel go way back and he should never forget where he came from. He never did, nor have I.

I am Malka Margolies' granddaughter, Malka Margolies.

ANDREA TRUPPIN

Andrea Truppin grew up in New York and lived in France for several years. In her work as a journalist, she focused on architecture, design, and decorative arts, writing for publications such as *Architecture, Interiors, Architectural Digest,* and *The New York Times.* Most recently, she served as editor-in-chief of *Modernism* magazine. She has also worked in documentary film and is currently employed by an international aid organization.

YOU SAY TOMATO

Andrea Truppin

My sister and I were born in New York, but when we were small, we spoke English with a South African accent, a lilting colonial cousin of the British one. I sang along with the English, Afrikaans, and Xhosa folk songs emanating scratchily from the heavy record my parents carried over from Cape Town on the *Queen Elizabeth* when they emigrated in 1955. During kindergarten rest hour, I claimed to the girl in the next cot that I spoke the foreign tongues, and proved it by whispering to her through the cardboard separator the memorized words: "N'kosi sikelele i Afrika," "Daar kom die Alibama," "Daar woon my Sarie Marais." I felt proud of my connection to what seemed a magical world—an impression surely nourished by my mother's oft-expressed homesickness.

Although I had never been to South Africa, the accent was part of me in the same way that I knew the clouds that floated in each afternoon to clothe Table Mountain. I knew Lion's Head and Devil's Peak, the pink spikes of the protea flowers, the hulking boulders at Clifton and the icy shock of the Atlantic below. I was a drinker of tea with cream crackers in a land of milk and cookies.

Once we started grade school, however, my sister and I borrowed the American accent to use with our classmates. But it gradually took over our speech until we couldn't help but use it at home as well. It was the accent that had horrified and confused my mother when she first arrived in New York – a vulgar accent, she complained, that made accomplished people sound illiterate. She began correcting us—"It's *going*, not *goy-ing*," "You are *taking* it, not *bringing* it." Cowed by this continual rebuke, we dared not abandon our ultimate tie to the fading linguistic world of our birth: the long, warm and elegant "ah," as in "dahnce" and "I cahn't." Americans said their "a" short and playfully; they "danced."

Over the years, the "ah" continued to reign in the apartment on East Ninetieth Street and on outings to Central Park, to the beach, the ballet—the world we shared with our parents. Except that gradually, tucked in among the American sounds, it no longer came out right. It twisted somehow into "ar," crept into "barthtub," and drifted into "I carn't." I remember the horror I felt when at school one day the tortured sound popped out of my mouth. I was thankful that no one noticed. More amazing was that my mother, with all her attentiveness to our speech, seemed deaf to this disgraceful deformation of her children's last overt tie to her homeland.

Recently, I found one of the daily-life tapes my gadget-mad father recorded. I am seven. My sister cries out, "Mommy, Andrea's not getting dressed!" My mother calls out to me, "Andrea, why aren't you getting dressed?" My plaintive voice responds, "But I carn't find my Darnskins!"

My mother shrieks, "Your WHAT?!!" I repeat, a bit unsure of myself this time, "my Darnskins," mispronouncing the Danskin brand name. "Why are you saying it like that?" my mother demands. I manage to peep out, "Darnskins, like to darnce."

Listening to this tape, I realize it has captured the very moment that my mother first noticed the ruin of the luckless "ah" that she had cupped gently in all its grace across the ocean to the New World. Fearful and lost amid the raucous bellowing of the city, she had treasured it as she read to us in the evening in our pink-and-white bedroom, confidently and lovingly expelling it with a soft, luxuriant breath into Hilaire Belloc, A.A. Milne, Dr. Seuss, and Edna St. Vincent Millay.

She resisted our accents, she told me later, for a long time. "Then what happened?" I asked. "Well," she answered, "I finally realized that you were American."

DAVID MASELLO

David Masello moved to New York more than thirty years ago from Evanston, Illinois, and he has made his living as a writer and editor ever since. He began his career as a nonfiction book editor at Simon & Schuster, then went on to hold senior editorial positions at many magazines, including *Travel & Leisure*, *Art and Antiques*, and *Town and Country*, where he was features editor. He's currently executive editor of *Milieu*, a magazine about design and architecture. He's a widely published essayist and poet, with pieces appearing in *The New York Times*, *Salon*, *Best American Essays*, and numerous literary and art magazines. His plays have been produced and performed by the Manhattan Repertory Theatre, Jewish Women's Theatre of Los Angeles, Big Apple Theater Festival, and Fresh Fruit Festival. He is the author of two books about art and architecture.

PRIOR TO TAKEOFF

David Masello

It was just as the pilot had said, prior to takeoff. He'd come through the cabin to tell two teenage brothers that over Cape Cod, we might be able to see fireworks. The evening was clear, the timing right. I thought it too late already—JFK's runways were edged with blue lights.

By the time we reached the Cape, a brushstroke of tangerine streaked the horizon, but on the ground it must've been dark. For yes, there they were—ballooning punctuations of exploding blooms along the coastlines and inland; fiefdoms of celebrations. I'd feared missing the July Fourth fireworks, but I was seeing more than in any year of my life.

To look at a landmass like the Cape from tens of thousands of feet, you realize the mapmakers in wooden-masted ships, spyglass to their eye, got it right centuries ago—so right that the tight spiral at Provincetown coils as a cliché of shapes.

While my fellow cab inmates, including the two boy brothers, were more interested in watching episodes of *Everybody Loves Raymond* than looking out at the world they were above, I looked down to the soundless explosions.

As we headed out into open ocean, I realized that none of this—the flight, my observance of every Fourth of July, late middle age—would *be*, had not *been* for the immigrant grandparents. Here I am, returning again, on holiday, to the homeland to which neither of them had ever returned. And on a jet, business class, a Brahms trio filling my headphones as I sip Chardonnay to get myself to sleep. The East Coast slides past like the vaudeville-act scenery my nana and papa might have watched, assuming they'd ever had a night off from stitching garments.

They came in steerage—twelve days was it? —a journey so claustrophobic for my boy grandfather that the phobia affected him his entire life. As an 80-year-old, on the drive with us from New Jersey to Chicago, he panics when we course the tunnels through the Alleghenies.

I'm the only one in business class who appears to be alone. Families monopolize the seating pods as if in their suburban Great Rooms, couples blindfolded, ear plugged, wrapped around each other. Unlike many trips, I leave on this one with at least someone, some people, about whom I can fantasize connecting at my return. I'm already thinking of the souvenirs I'll buy each, their gratitude when I hand them wrapped gifts. How self-indulgent of me, though, when I think of the grandparents who came as children, my 12-year-old grandfather alone, never again seeing his parents. I'll be hearing their dialect in Campania, that same shh-ing sound my father used when he and I would try to speak Italian, mine formal, his not, both of us choosing instead the language of laughter in which we were fluent.

When I arrived in the Amalfi Coast town that embraces sea and mountains, I shot a video of the two-minute-and-thirty-eight-second maze-like walk from my rented apartment to the piazza. Passing a Christmas-bulb-traced Mary shrine, hearing the clinks of forks twirling pasta, greetings of *salve* from my neighbors, little kids cradling soccer balls as they say *ciao*. A boy lived with his family below me and whenever I descended the staircase, he'd emerge with his dog. He was friendly, not effusive, purposeful, taking off down the steps, flip-flops snapping. My last morning, I walked to the rocky beach and found the boy there, walking another dog. Oh, so this is what he does, walks other people's dogs, patient in letting each one sniff and lap from the fountain.

He's a considerate boy, with keys to many houses. I think of my grandfather at his age, leaving, the door to his house closing.

This is how fast the world changes, something you realize even prior to landing. I had been afraid of missing the holiday explosions, but if you want light, you find it.

EDWARD McCANN

Edward McCann is an award winning writer/producer and the founder and editor of **650**, a literary forum that celebrates the spoken word with live events in New York City and elsewhere. A longtime contributing editor to *Country Living*, his features and essays have been published in many literary journals, anthologies, and national magazines, including *Milieu, Better Homes & Gardens, Good Housekeeping, The Irish Echo, The Sun, and others.* His essay, "Pregnant Again," was selected for the anthology, *Listen To Your Mother*, published by Penguin, and he's recently completed a memoir about the search for his missing nephew. A member of New York City-based Artists Without Walls, he lives and writes in New York's Hudson River Valley.

ACKNOWLEDGMENTS

In addition to the contributors to this volume, we thank the **New Rochelle Council on the Arts** for its generous support of 650, and for stimulating and encouraging the study and presentation of the performing and fine arts. Throughout the year, NRCA sponsors many exhibitions, theatrical productions, dance recitals, film screenings, lectures, and concert series.
NewRochelleArts.org

We thank **The New Rochelle Public Library** for hosting a 650 live event in its beautiful Ossie Davis Theater. The library offers a comprehensive collection that includes retrospective and current materials, up-to-date technology by which information can be accessed, and a wide range of community services and programs tailored to a diverse audience.
NRPL.org

Nancy Manocherian's the cell has supported 650 from its inception. A twenty-first century salon in the heart of New York City, their mission is to support the arts and to incubate new works, and the cell made its beautiful performance space available to 650 as we were finding our way. The cell: To mine the mind, pierce the heart, and awaken the soul.
TheCellTheatre.org

Artists Without Walls was created to inspire, uplift and unite people and communities of diverse cultures through the pursuit of artistic achievement, and has supported and encouraged 650 from its beginnings. Artists Without Walls: No Limits. No Walls. No Boundaries.
ArtistsWithoutWalls.com

READ650.COM

INFO @READ650.COM
FACEBOOK.COM/READ650